Holy Places

The Golden Temple

and Other Sikh Holy Places

Victoria Parker

For information, address the publisher:
Raintree, 100 N. LaSalle, Suite 1200, Chicago, IL 60602

Design by Joanna Sapwell and StoryBooks
Printed and bound in China.

07 06 05 04 03
10 9 8 7 6 5 4 3 2 1

Library of Congress Cataloging-in-Publication Data

Parker, Victoria.
   The Golden Temple / Victoria Parker.
      p. cm. -- (Holy places)
   Summary: An introduction to Sikhism which focuses on the
   holy sites of the religion.
   Includes bibliographical references and index.
   ISBN 0-7398-6079-8 (HC), 1-4109-0052-5 (Pbk.)
   1. Golden Temple (Amritsar, India)--Juvenile literature.
   2. Temples, Sikh--India--Amritsar--Juvenile literature. 3. Amritsar (India)--Religious life and customs--Juvenile literature.
   4. Sikhism--India--Amritsar--Juvenile literature.   [1. Golden
   Temple (Amritsar, India) 2. Sikhism.]   I. Title. II. Series.
   BL2018.36.A472G647 2003
   294.6'35'0954552--dc21

2002014389

Acknowledgments
The Publishers would like to thank the following for permission to reproduce photographs: Associated Press
p. 10; Christine Osbourne Pictures p. 27; Circa Photo Library pp. 16, 17, 18, 26; Corbis p. 25; Dinodia Picture
Agency pp. 9, 12; Gopinder Kaur p. 28; Harjinder Singh Sagoo p. 29; Trip/B Dhanjal pp. 20, 22; Trip/H Rogers
pp. 5, 6, 7, 8, 11, 13, 14, 15, 19, 21, 23, 24.

Cover photograph reproduced with permission of Trip/H Rogers.

Every effort has been made to contact copyright holders of any material reproduced in this book.
Any omissions will be rectified in subsequent printings if notice is given to the Publisher.

Contents

Words printed in bold letters, **like this**, are explained in the Glossary on page 30.

What Is the Golden Temple?

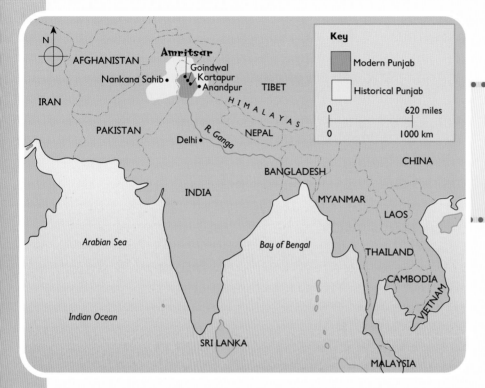

One of the world's most famous **temples** is in Amritsar, in the **Punjab,** an area in northwest India. The temple's name is the "Harmandir Sahib," which means God's temple. Most people just call it the Golden Temple.

The Golden Temple was built over 400 years ago in the middle of a **sacred** pool. People believed that the waters had the power to heal sick people. A splendid city sprang up around the Golden Temple with houses, shops, schools, and hospitals. This city was called Amritsar.

Other religions

Not all people in India are Sikhs. There are many who are **Hindu, Buddhist,** and **Muslim.** People become full members of the Sikh religion in a special ceremony. They share some food and a drink called **amrit.** This is to show that God thinks all people are important and that people of all religions should be friends.

Every year, thousands of people from different countries make long journeys to visit the Golden Temple. Some come just to see the beautiful place, but many more people come there to worship God. They pray and do good deeds to help others. These men and women are called Sikhs, because they follow a religion called Sikhism. Long ago, a Sikh leader, or **Guru,** gave instructions for the Golden Temple to be built.

The outside of the Golden Temple is covered with gold.

Who Are the Sikhs?

Nanak thought that people of different religions should be friends and should not fight.

The word "Sikh" means follower. Sikhs are followers of a **holy** man called Nanak. He lived over 500 years ago. Nanak's family were **Hindus,** but he had a lot of **Muslim** friends. Stories say that when Nanak was about 30 years old, he walked into a river and disappeared. Amazingly, several days later Nanak walked out of the waters alive and well! Nanak said that he had been with God.

God had told Nanak that following a **religion** was not as important as living a good and truthful life helping others. From then on, Nanak was known as **Guru** Nanak.

Guru Nanak traveled around speaking God's teachings as poems. One of his Muslim friends, named Mardana, wrote music for the poems so that they could be sung as **hymns.**

Just before Guru Nanak died, he asked a man called Guru Angad to take over. Guru Angad wrote down Guru Nanak's hymns so no one would ever forget them. The next Guru, Amar Das, chose 22 women and men to travel as **missionaries,** spreading Guru Nanak's beliefs. The fourth Guru, Ram Das, decided that Sikhs should have their own city so he built a town called Chak Ramdasspur. This was later renamed Amritsar by his son.

Nowadays, Sikh families live not just in India, but all over the world.

What Is the Sacred Pool?

Pilgrims often bathe in the sacred pool before entering the temple to pray.

People say that the land on which Amritsar was built was given to the Sikhs by a **Muslim** leader called **Emperor** Akbar. It is a special place for people of many different **faiths,** because of the **sacred** pool there. Sikhs believe that the second **Guru** had an illness that was healed with an **herb** that grew near the pool. **Hindu** stories tell how their god Rama was killed in a battle, but was brought back to life by drinking the water. **Buddhists** say that their leader, the Buddha, also visited the pool once.

The third Guru, Amar Das, thought the sacred pool should be made larger. His followers dug it wider and deeper. Then, under the fourth Guru, Ram Das, many Sikhs helped to build homes, lay roads, dig wells, and open shops around it.

The fifth Guru, Arjan, made Amritsar look like it does today. The whole pool was lined with bricks, and a mighty **temple** was built in the middle of it. This is the temple that today we call the Golden Temple.

This is how Amritsar looks today.

9

Amritsar After the Gurus

At the time of **Guru** Arjan, who lived between 1563 and 1606, the **emperor** of India was a **Muslim.** He wanted the Sikhs of Amritsar to become Muslims. The next Guru, Har Gobind, moved away to try to stop the problems. But things grew worse. From then on, the Gurus no longer lived at Amritsar. The tenth Guru, Gobind Singh, was the last. The trouble became so bad that he formed a Sikh army.

For the next 100 years, Sikhs were in a lot of danger. New rulers who wanted to kill the Sikhs took over India. At first, men and women fled from Amritsar. Later, they

> This is one of the marble walkways inside the Golden Temple.

returned and banded together in small fighting groups and built forts to protect the city. Many Sikh war-leaders built big headquarters called bungas. As the fighting stopped, the bungas became grander, like palaces. Important people such as scientists, artists, and teachers came to stay at the bungas and study around the **temple** and the pool. The city began to grow and flourish once more.

Pilgrims bathe in the sacred pool. You can see one of the bungas in the back.

What Does the Golden Temple Look Like?

The Golden **Temple** is one of the most beautiful buildings in the world. The workers who built it were not just Sikhs, but **Muslims** and **Hindus** too. There are many carvings on the outside walls. A lot of the decorations have hidden meanings. Carvings of animals and birds remind Sikhs that life can be difficult at times, but flowers and fruit mean that life can be beautiful as well.

The temple lies right at the center of the **sacred** pool. There is a long, wide bridge that leads across the water. The temple has four doors, one on each side, to show that people from all parts of the world are welcome. Many Sikhs wash in the sacred pool before they enter the temple. They also take off their shoes and leave them at the entrance as a sign of respect.

Many precious and expensive materials were used to decorate the Golden Temple.

Every 50 years, over a million Sikhs come to Amritsar to help clean out the pool. This type of help is called sewa, which means "service." Sikhs believe that sewa is a way of worshiping God. Other forms of sewa are cooking and cleaning at home or at the **gurdwara,** and helping sick or poor people.

Inside, the temple is decorated with more carvings, patterns in gold and silver, and beautiful wall paintings called frescoes. One room glitters and sparkles because it is covered in thousands of tiny pieces of colored glass.

Every inch of the Temple is beautifully decorated.

What Is the Sikh Holy Book?

Sikhs show a lot of respect for their holy book, the Guru Granth Sahib.

The **Guru Granth Sahib** is a collection of **hymns** written from the words of **Guru** Nanak by the other Gurus and **Hindu** and **Muslim holy** men.

When the tenth Guru, Gobind Singh, was dying, he announced that the next Guru would not be a man, but would be the holy book instead. It was given the title the Guru Granth Sahib. Sikhs believe it is the word of God.

Every **gurdwara** in the world has a Guru Granth Sahib. Each copy is exactly the same, with 1,430 pages. When the Guru Granth Sahib is not being used, it is kept in a special room of its own and covered with a beautiful cloth called a **rumala**.

This is the first verse of the Guru Granth Sahib, which was written by Guru Nanak. It shows that Sikhs see God as a spirit, one who is not male or female:

> *There is only one God*
> *Whose name is Truth*
> *Who is the Creator*
> *Who is without fear*
> *Who is without hate*
> *Who does not die*
> *Who is not born*
> *Who is the light*
> *Who is known by the kindness of the Guru.*

During a Sikh **service,** a man or woman called a **Granthi** reads from the Guru Granth Sahib. Then, there are talks to explain the readings. Sometimes, the Granthi waves a fan called a chauri over the Guru Granth Sahib to show respect. This sort of fan was used in the past in India to fan the kings.

There is a special ceremony to carry the Guru Granth Sahib to and from the worship room.

Eating Together

At the Golden Temple, there is a big kitchen and a space for eating, called a **langar.** Every **gurdwara** in the world has a langar.

The langar has two uses. First, at the end of a Sikh **service,** everyone is offered a piece of **holy** food called **karah prasad.** This is a type of sweet pudding. It is made by cooks who say **hymns** from the **Guru Granth Sahib** while they are preparing it. Just before the karah prasad is taken to the worship room, the cooks **bless** it. Each Sikh cups their hands to receive a piece and they bow before they eat it.

Worshipers are eating in the langar at the Golden Temple.

Karah prasad

To make a pudding like karah prasad, ask a grown-up for help with these instructions. First, wash your hands. Then, melt about 7 oz. of butter in a saucepan. Add 7 oz. of flour and stir the mixture for 5 minutes over a low heat. Mix in 7 oz. of sugar and half a cup of water. Stir the mixture slowly until it thickens. Leave it to cool and set. Then, it is ready to share!

The langar is also used to prepare a meal that everybody shares after the service. This meal is also called langar. The meal is free and everyone is welcome, whether they are Sikh or not.

Guru Nanak thought that eating together was important because it showed that everyone was friends. Sikhs believe that in order to love God you must love all of God's people, no matter what their beliefs are.

These British Sikhs are sharing a meal at their own gurdwara.

A Day at the Golden Temple

Worshipers arrive at the Golden **Temple** at two or three o'clock in the morning. They sing **hymns** until four or five. Then, the **Guru Granth Sahib** is brought from its resting place. Several Sikhs carry it in a golden box.

The Guru Granth Sahib is placed on the **takht.** A **Granthi,** or reader, lets the **holy** book fall open at any page and reads the first verse that appears. Sikhs believe that this is God's advice for the day. The worshipers say a special prayer called the Ardas, and **karah prasad** is given out to end the **service.**

Here, a Granthi is reading from the Guru Granth Sahib.

Sikhs come to the Golden Temple all day. People read aloud from the Guru Granth Sahib. Worshipers sit and listen, and then they join others in the **langar** to eat.

Late in the evening, there is a final prayer ceremony. Then, the Guru Granth Sahib is wrapped up. A Granthi carries it on his head to its resting place. The worshipers then clean and sweep the Temple.

Gurdwaras all over the world follow the same daily pattern.

The day's verse is written on a notice board so people can read it.

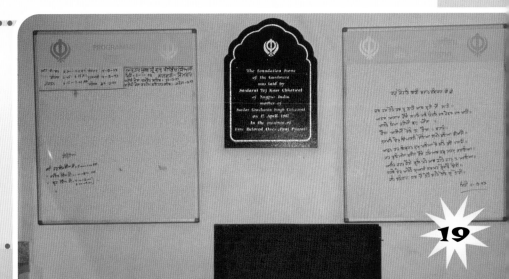

What Festivals Do Sikhs Celebrate?

Sikhs celebrate many festivals. Three important celebrations are held at the same time as **Hindu** festivals.

Baisakhi is held at Indian New Year on April 13 or 14. Hindus thank God for the spring harvest. Sikhs celebrate how **Guru** Gobind Singh chose five men to form a special group called the **Khalsa.** These Sikhs promised to follow strict rules for the rest of their lives.

Holi is another ancient Hindu spring festival. Sikhs call it Hola Mohalla and celebrate it the day after Holi. Guru Gobind Singh decided that Sikh soldiers would celebrate it with competitions in

Many Sikhs choose to become a member of the Khalsa, like this man.

The Khalsa

Members of the Khalsa wear five things that begin with K. Kachera is underwear like shorts. A kara is a steel bracelet. The circle shape shows that God has no beginning and no end. A kirpan is a small sword. It reminds Sikhs to fight evil. Kesh means hair. Sikhs are not allowed to cut their hair. A kanga is a little comb that Sikhs wear to keep their long hair tidy.

horseriding, archery, and wrestling. The competitions still take place today in a town called Anandpur.

Diwali is the Festival of Light. Hindus celebrate good winning out over evil. Sikhs celebrate the bravery of the sixth Guru, Har Gobind. The Guru was once thrown into prison. When the **emperor** finally released him, the Guru said he would not go unless the other prisoners were let out, too. The Guru cleverly saved 52 other people and returned to Amritsar in triumph.

Sikhs and Hindus light hundreds of candles at the festival of Diwali.

21

Sikh Celebrations

Sikhs hold special celebrations to mark the birthdays and the deaths of the ten **Gurus.** These festivals are called gurpurbs. At **gurdwaras** around the world, people take turns reading the **Guru Granth Sahib** from beginning to end. This takes two whole days and nights. The long reading is called an Akhand Path. Musicians play and worshipers join in with the **hymns.**

Hundreds of Sikhs get together to parade through the streets. Five people usually lead the way, reminding everyone of the first five members of the **Khalsa.** The Guru Granth Sahib is carried on its throne. It is decorated

These British Sikhs are celebrating a gurpurb.

DID YOU KNOW?

Sikhs sometimes send each other greeting cards on the birthday of a Guru. The cards often have a design called the Khanda on them. The Khanda stands for God and the rules of the Sikh religion. You can also see the Khanda on the yellow flag that flies outside every gurdwara.

with flowers and banners and everyone sings hymns as it passes. The crowds are given gifts of sweets.

Special celebrations take place at Amritsar on the Gurus' birthdays and also on the day when the Guru Granth Sahib was first placed in the Golden **Temple.** The Golden Temple usually has silver gates, but for these festivals they are replaced by gold ones. The whole building is lit up on the outside. Inside, all the temple treasures are put on view for people to see. Thousands of Sikhs come to celebrate, and huge feasts are prepared for everyone.

Every gurdwara flies a flag like this one.

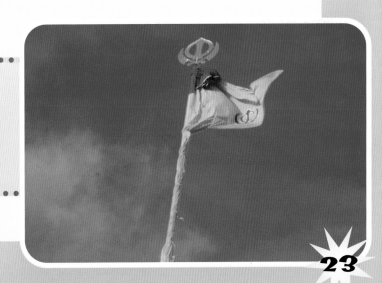

23

What Is the Shrine of Baba Dip Singh?

These Sikhs are showing respect for the hero Baba Dip Singh.

The Golden **Temple** is not the only **holy** building for Sikhs in Amritsar. There are many other Sikh **shrines** in the city. An important one is the shrine of Baba Dip Singh.

Baba Dip Singh lived in Amritsar about 250 years ago. He worked writing out copies of the **Guru Granth Sahib,** which was a job that required great skill. At this time, the **Punjab** was ruled by the **emperor** of India, Ahmad Shah. Ahmad Shah was a **Muslim** who did not like Sikhs. He did a terrible thing. He blew up the Golden Temple and filled the **sacred** pool with dead cows. Sikhs everywhere were horrified and angry.

Baba Dip Singh swore that he would fight Ahmad Shah's army and then rebuild the Golden Temple. Over 5,000 Sikhs promised to help him.

Baba Dip Singh and his army fought their way to Amritsar to face Emperor Ahmad Shah. Most of the Sikhs were killed. Baba Dip Singh himself was badly injured. He managed to reach the sacred pool, but then he collapsed and died. Today, Sikhs place flowers on the spot where Baba Dip Singh lay. A shrine for him has been built nearby, and a light is kept burning there day and night.

A picture of the Hindu god Ganesh on a door on the Hindu Durgianna Temple.

More Holy Places in Amritsar

Some of the Sikh **holy** places in Amritsar are not buildings. Many Sikhs go to a pool called Ramsar Pool. This is where **Guru** Arjan sat when he was putting together the **Guru Granth Sahib**.

Sikhs also visit a special tree at the Golden **Temple**. The tree is where Baba Buddha used to sit and give teachings. Baba Buddha was a man who knew Guru Nanak. He lived for such a long time that he was friends with the next four Gurus too. Baba Buddha was given the honor of being the very first **Granthi**.

The Dukhbhanjani Ber tree stands in the Golden Temple.

There is another tree in Amritsar that Sikhs believe is **sacred.** A story tells about a very poor woman named Rajni who came from a town called Patti. She lived before the Golden Temple was built. Rajni's husband was very ill so she took him to holy places all over India asking God to cure him.

Rajni arrived at the sacred pool of Amritsar without knowing that people said it could heal the sick. She left her husband under a tree while she went to beg for food. While Rajni was gone, her husband bathed in the pool and was made well again! Sikhs call the tree where he lay Dukhbhanjani Ber, which means "the tree that destroys sorrow."

The Panja Sahib Temple is where Guru Nanak taught.

27

Everyday Sikh Life

Today, there are Sikh communities in many different countries. Their **gurdwaras** do not always look the same. Some are built in a special way. Others are set up in old buildings like big houses. All gurdwaras have a worship hall, a room for the **Guru Granth Sahib,** and a **langar.**

Sikhs all over the world worship in the same way. When they visit their gurdwara, they kneel before the Guru Granth Sahib to show respect. They sometimes bring gifts of money or food. Men and women sit on the floor on different sides of the gurdwara, but they are on the same level and they have the same space. This is to show that all people are equally important. Children sit on either side.

This is the inside of a gurdwara in Britain.

The gurdwara is the center of Sikh life. Sikh families celebrate all of their important events at the gurdwara. Weddings are held here. New babies are named in the gurdwara. For this, the Guru Granth Sahib is opened at any page. The very first letter on that page is given as the first letter of the baby's name. A special event for boys also takes place here. Young boys keep their long hair tied in a topknot. When they are older, they go to the gurdwara for a special ceremony to tie their first **turban.**

This Sikh boy is taking part in his turban-tying ceremony.

29

Glossary

amrit special sugary liquid that people drink in a ceremony when they become full members of the Sikh religion

bless ask God to make somebody or something holy

Buddhist person who follows the spiritual teaching of the Buddha

Christian person who follows the teachings of Jesus

church building where Christians worship God

emperor ruler of an empire, which is a large area made up of different countries and peoples

faiths different religions or beliefs about God

Granthi man or woman who reads from the Sikh holy book and looks after it

gurdwara Sikh name for a temple

Guru Sikh teacher or holy person

Guru Granth Sahib Sikh holy book, which is treated as a living person. It is also known as the Adi Granth (First Book).

gutka shortened version of the Guru Granth Sahib containing the most important daily prayers and hymns. Sikhs keep this for personal use at home.

herb plant with a distinctive smell that is often used in cooking. Some are believed to have healing powers.

Hindu person who follows the Hindu religion

holy having to do with God

hymns songs sung to worship God

karah prasad sweet food that is blessed and given out to Sikhs at worship

Khalsa Sikhs who choose to follow the strict rules of the religion. These rules are also called Khalsa.

langar food that is free for all Sikhs who come to a gurdwara to worship. Langar is also the name given to the kitchen where this food is cooked.

missionaries people whose job is to travel and teach people about God

mosque building where Muslims go to worship God

Muslim person who follows a religion called Islam, based on the teachings of a prophet named Muhammad (pbuh)

Punjab place in India where the Sikh religion began

Punjabi language spoken by people in the Punjab

religion organized way of worshiping God

rumala special cloth in which the Guru Granth Sahib is wrapped when it is not being used

sacred something believed to be special to God

service organized gathering of worshipers

shrine place of worship that is special for a certain holy person or thing

takht throne where the Guru Granth Sahib is placed during worship

temple building where people worship God

turban length of cloth that Sikh men wear wrapped around their heads

Index